The Angel and
the Heretic

SAINT JULIAN PRESS

POETRY SERIES

"Britt Posmer has obviously crossed the threshold into the state of non abiding. In a clear, liberated and liberating, unconventional voice, she gives us "the raw seduction of real love." She has traversed the underbelly of life and knows the dense and dark caverns of the human condition. Like every true shaman, she has returned to share her discoveries. Britt pulls words like arrows from an invisible quiver, while pirouetting beneath a moonless sky. Yes, a luminous quiver hewn during hours and hours-becoming-years of internal exploration. Britt is Artemis, the "huntress pregnant with god," who expresses the direct approach interwoven with unapologetic, Deep feminine, primordial wisdom!"

~ Rashani Réa, artist, activist, intimist; author of *Beyond Brokenness*, *Shimmering Birthless* and *Moonlight on a Night Moth's Wing*.

"The poet in crisis (our crisis) can, like Basho and the Zen masters, remove the subject, the "I," from the naked suchness of the dusty crumb. Then the poem is a verbal still-life, capturing a single moment unoccupied by the human self: the essence of Haiku. Or the poet can retain the "I" and fill it with tears, with the pangs of all her unborn children, with every stifled uncertain abused and human voice, even the voice of the homeless angel.

Britt Posmer has chosen to retain the "I," but an empty "i" (we must think of Keat's "negative capability") who takes into its vacuous orb the bodies of hurt children, fallen stars, muted women, mothers, half burnt seeds, mouths bursting in silent zeros of pain. She finds a single voice for the animal and angel in us, giving her poems the irony of wholeness, the grief that germinates eternal beauty.

Britt is a poet of revelation, exposing a secret alchemy by which the touch of human bodies is transmuted to the light by which God sees. Read these poems again and again. They will never be old."

~Alfred K. LaMotte, whose books include *Wounded Bud: Poems for Meditation* and *Shimmering Birthless: a Confluence of Verse and Image* with Rashani Réa.

"In conversations with angels we find a shared angst, a beautiful blending of a number of traditions; koans and angels co-exist. On the page many worlds collide. This first book of poetry by Britt Posmer is a call to compassion not only for ourselves, our bodies and for each other but also those considered divine; the ones we turn to.

"the ones who cry don't disappear
just because we are tired of looking"

We are taken on a journey of shared grief, "Behind our ears we are all tucking cemetery flowers." An exploration of the places where angels play cards and our "body is the path of homecoming".

~ Jónína Kirton, author of *page as bone ~ ink as blood.*

"Britt's poems dance with elegance and great courage and they speak to my heart directly and fearlessly. They are not mental exercise. They are rather deep pointers to what cannot be said with words. Their simplicity and clarity is like music we hear when we turn our face towards the ocean of life."

~Guthema Roba, author of *Wake Up and Roar — Poetry for Meditation and Awakening*

The Angel and the Heretic

Poems

By

Britt Posmer

Saint Julian Press

Houston

Published by Saint Julian Press, Inc.

2053 Cortlandt, Suite 200

Houston, Texas 77008

www.saintjulianpress.com

ISBN-13: 978-0-9965231-1-0

ISBN-10: 0996523111

Library of Congress Control Number: 2015944465

Cover Art: The Angel and the Heretic
24 x 20, Acrylic On Canvas
by Britt Posmer

"For the Burning Ones"

TABLE OF CONTENTS

PREFACE

We are mistaken if we believe that children are incapable of genuine mystical experience. The heart of awakening is not about special states or visions granted only to a chosen few, but the unadorned simplicity of recognizing the fresh and expansive wonder of who we effortlessly are. This can happen to anyone, at any time, in any stage of life. Around the age of five, I had a series of "previews" into this fundamental nature that set an unalterable course for the coming years. Somehow, I was left with the unshakeable knowing that my life would be divided in two; at a certain point, I knew not when, the orientation of my being would shift completely. It was nothing to worry about, and there was nothing to be done. What was not made clear at that time was the *between*, the act of waiting as one existence fell away with another not yet here, while the sense of waiting *for* dropped away entirely. Nor did I understand what it would mean to be carried by hope, into abject hopelessness, and then beyond both, until even the original promise had been forgotten.

The poems in this collection are written from the ambiguity and groundlessness of a not-knowing as total as the love pulling the invisible thread of the New into form. In 2009, I was plunged into a period of catastrophic illness and collapse that left me hovering near death for the next two years. Recovery has been slow and continues even now, along with the painstaking conversations between body, psyche, heart, and spirit that constitute the soul-making of a truly human life. During this time, Love revealed itself in ever more radical ways until I finally realized that this immense gifting was ultimately the last great Heresy. The invitation to wake as the whole of who we are smashes all of our sacred cows. It roots out each paralyzed limitation and defense with fearsome kindness and undermines every preference we might hold as to the form of its appearing. Brokenness is not an obstacle, but a requirement. The tangles of our most profound agony and confusion are liberated by the singleness of its boundless compassion into the pure substance of homecoming.

This is a book about finding yourself in the nakedness of Being, finding the world in the smallest fragments of your humanity, and finding the holy in a shared hiddenness that remains perpetually self-secret yet leaves its traces dancing everywhere in wild and playful abundance. These words are also a portal into the living field of courage: the courage to take up your seat and offer your gifts without shame, the courage to speak what has gone too long unspeakable, the courage to bow to a handful of fragments, fractals of wholeness, splinters of grace.

All that is written here is inseparable from the Space in which, and of which, it was composed. You are invited to encounter reading as resonance and as the inescapable responsiveness of mutual indwelling. Savor the shape and weight of language, remembering that poetry is a heart-call to embodied participation and the very Body of our seamless love, poured out to be consumed.

May 2015

"See, I have sown fire into the
cosmos, and I shall guard it carefully
until it blazes."

Logion 10, *The Gospel of Thomas*

"They tried to bury us. They didn't know we were seeds."
~ Mexican proverb

The Angel and
the Heretic

PASSAGE

I am not
your vanilla saint. I am
this miracle:

corpse trailing a comet's tail
of ecstatic flesh.

Attended by your love,
I'm free

to roam the mystic hallways
of my childhood faith. My body
is the path of homecoming.

Travel me.

SWORD

It was not your intention
that the nearness of your love
should render me inconsolable.

But you sheathed your existence
in my flesh, and now,

with every movement my body
cries out, torn against the steel edge
of your unclad beauty.

THE REALITY OF ME

exists
so far outside
of language that I
belly-crawl
a thousand times
a day
down the long
darkness
of my throat
to borrow
a word
for a hand
a foot
a pair of eyes
a sweeping flank
to create
for myself
the body
that I need

LOVE NOTE

On the back of a crumpled grocery list,
I wrote a love note to the world

and left it beside the coffeepot,
where it would be found upon waking.

It said:
My Precious Earth,

You are my Pieta.
Everywhere and always

I carry your broken body
in my arms. I live within

the long and terrible shadow
of your Light.

PRAYER

She was believed to be devout,
though she spent the creeping hours
on her knees simply because she
had been struck too many times to stand.

No one thought to question
this was not necessarily prayer.

SUBURBAN NATIVITY

This year
we bought a disposable
Jesus.

He'll be recycled, of course,
among the discarded
pine boughs and empty
cat food cans

half-filled with melting snow.

The child is not
so unique.
Plenty of babies are left

outside in the cold. Still,

I do not think
the over-exposed glow
in the center of his plastic chest

is the Light that he meant.

MOUTHBROODING

I wait for the man with the green
shadow, who will swallow me on
the scarlet couch of his tongue.
He will be my father-fish,
carrying me to freedom in his mouth,
spitting my wriggling form
back into the sea.

WENDY

She left a note
for those who would pursue
her. "Don't wade into the Sea
if you cannot swim in deep water
or if you are afraid
of sharks,
or shipwrecks, or
sunless silences
that stretch for miles."

The shores are filled with
children who play at being
mermaids and the sailors
who bury themselves
in a fish's salty skin.

Wendy said, "Don't
follow me, Peter.

In real life, you drown."

GENDER STUDIES

adam and
adam and
adam and
adam and
adam and
oh yes

eve

HOW TO CALL A UNICORN

Stretch out your hand,
unmoving,

that I might have
the pleasure of approach.

Then see - proud
creature! -

how I stride
towards you,

bow to rest my cheek
against your palm,

and love you,

because your fingers
do not close,

because you hold me
only by your breathing.

WHOSE

Sometimes there is a pause
and a space
and a holding
and I

wonder whose tears
have dropped upon my open palm
or the back of whose neck
I have secretly kissed

while they thought it was the wind.

THE NIGHT YOU CAME AS MICHAEL THE ARCHANGEL

I loved you most
among the avenging angels,

You,

who retained your darkness,
wherein to be named

was not to know.

You alone
had the courage

to remain a question,

an eternal listening
too enraptured by space

to number the stars.

You were the field
where battles raged

and fell, where I was

God, and I was mud,
and I was flesh, and I

was not. You were everything.

And for once, I had
what I most wanted:

to be empty.

CRONING

Why waste my time
idolizing lost youth?

I am an old, blind woman
growing the gift of extra hands.

MADONNA

We mistake her.

This silent, inward turning
is no mute docility.

Through absolute submission
to the Love waiting to take form within her,
she has become wholly,
undomesticably

wild.

Every lie now knows:
She is the most dangerous woman in the world.

SWAN

I was a bird
caught at dusk

a swan
with one white wing

calamity and Call

ENOUGH

I am an oyster.

Inside a tight-lipped mouth,
a lavender-gray blossom
of regret rests

upon the soft, pink belly
of my tongue. No worries
enter here, rocking

on the salt-tides of the
breath, sweeping blood
through its arterial reefs.

It is my nature to make pearls.

(This is how it feels
to be enough.)

THE ACTIVITY OF WAITING

Eyes drawn upwards, balanced precariously
on a limb far too small, I am weightless,

without space, absent of dimension.

I am listening for the wind to tell me when to lean,
to topple forward into its outstretched arms.

THE ABANDONMENT OF STATES

I am done
chasing after your
red ecstasies
and cloud-blue bliss.

Come to me naked,
unadorned by feeling.

Come to me now,
in a way that can
never be lost.

TARA

I'm trying to tell you something.

Beneath the world's optimistic facade,
behind the slow smile of soul-death,

the ones who cry don't disappear
just because we're tired of looking.

DIVINE PHYSICIAN

The wound knows its own medicine.

GENESIS 32

I understand Jacob
why he wouldn't
let go and how
wrapping your legs
around the holy
leaves a mark
even as it
heals.

YOURS

No one can teach you
the language that is yours,
the language not yet spoken.

No one can give you the courage
for that which is rising inside you
that has never been.

REFUGE

I take refuge
on the floor
of the heart's
chapel,
between
creaking pews
smelling
of cracked leather
and fallen hymnals,
bound blue,
like broken eggshells
too small
to hold love's
longing
in its flight
to God.

Prayer is fetal.
Head to
knees,
completing
a circle
of departure.

I have already
gambled
with my death
and won.

INSTRUCTIONS TO THE DEVOTEE

Cultivate an aptitude for prostration.

MORE

There is something more than happiness.
I do not know

how to name it, but it makes my cells shine,
and I do not call it light,

but a secret envy I share with the sun,
a brighter star in which we disappear, transparent.

RHINOCEROS

There was a rhinoceros
on the roof.

You insisted it was a
pigeon (what difference?

they're both gray as the stones
in the driveway).

The truth that you refuse
will deprive you

of the miraculous,
and...

the ceiling will still fall.

DESCENT

The
Body
has
become
a sword
at whose
feet
every
Lie
falls.

BEATITUDES

Blessed are the man and woman
who can speak plainly of brutality
without losing their humanity.
Blessed are

we who have found God
in his priest hole, sheltered
in the midst of rage, or crouched
beneath the floorboards like a rabbit
(dark eyes infinite and shining),
twitching his nose. Blessed is

the love that never heard the word
and thus escaped its own confinement,
and blessed are

the names I call you in my unknown heart,
the ones that sound like fire
and the sharp gasp of the collapsing branch
as it is taken.

HER

I am in love
with a woman whose body
is the collapse of nations
and whose voice
speaks of an ocean

with no moon.

As long as you continue
to confuse sentimentality
with love
you will never understand
my need of her.

I WONDER

I wonder if you see it yet
how some of us beg
to be broken
and to be unburdened
by the magnitude of loss

of the accumulations
of an ill-fitting and fictional

Me.
I wonder

if you've tasted the great
madness of confinement
and heard that the feral voice
at the heart of all your self-destruction
was fundamentally the sound

of your own astonishing fecundity.
I wonder if you've stopped
betraying death and found him
faithful. I wonder if you've lost
count of the untold flavors

hidden in your tears.
I wonder

if you can detect the scent
that lightning leaves
behind as it singes the ground

and I

wonder if you know
you've touched my life
the same.

THE BACK ROOM

I've been hanging out in the back room
with the angels, drinking and dealing cards,
trying to decide which death to play.

(The sacrifices of past and future
are linked; we move forward not knowing
who we are.)

Boots on the table, Michael arches his brows
and blows smoke rings at me in the shape of a question.

I'm all in.

Give me the raw seduction of real love,
and in my heart I'll build for you a monument
to the frailty that makes us immortal.

CONTINENTS

All continents are wanderers.
Some drift.

Some dismember themselves
in the cataclysm

of their love.

Before Daybreak

I was not ready for you.
I could not sit so near
my own Aliveness.

This was not exactly a refusal.

My body got caught in the Grail gate,
holding it ajar. We prayed for time.

There are purple handprints
on my breasts from where shame
clutched and would not let go.

Do you remember how you invited it
like a badger you pulled from a dark hole
by its tail and then left

the room, locking me inside?
Haven't we all been Peter, torn

between remaining near Love
and staying unrecognized, muttering

our ass-covering denials? We can
grieve, but what choice did we have?
It was not yet day.

FOUND

A profusion of nicety hamstrings
genuine praise.

We never learned that we could harm
through sweetness clung to
when the gods called for truth in blood
and the blooms of arterial roses
that pacified worlds
with their uncompromising ardor.
You cannot make black white

simply because you lack the language
to speak their difference.

You will be found

when Love puts on her homespun
dress, and covered in embers and burning
ash, sweeps the floor of your inmost dwelling.

GONE

So quiet now
I have disappeared

but you would not
know it I am

that close to you.

DAUGHTER OF EVE

Sweet girl, you are not awake
until you've known
the hostility of apples. Teeth bared,
we are dancing.

I have offered my body
to despair. Before there was a tree,
we were all hanging, arms outstretched,
flung, frozen into pale branches,
while grateful graces with folded hands
sat primly, ankles crossed beneath the table.

If Woman is a vessel, I am
a ship,

carrying the Death Child,
like holy Mary, or Buddha's mother,
who dreamed that a white elephant
had slid into her womb.

We dig with nails and tusks
and broken claws forgetful
of their wildness,
to hold in our hands the pain
that called to us below the ground.

Pray now
for eyes like lanterns,
or better still for blindness

that paints on your skin
a map
only your naked heart can read.

LIGHT FROM BURNING

Unconsciousness calls to unconsciousness
in a way we can mistake as love to love,
bearing some of the same qualities
of intimacy.

Whenever it was false, her feet turned blue.

The children that we were
huddled around garbage cans
that burned with the memory
of mothers we never had.
Lost boys clung to orphan girls
with matches to spare.

From an abandoned doorway, she watched
the shadows flicker across the face
of someone she knew. Her heart whispered,
"The foundations of the world

are neither dark, nor bright," as the words
froze like eyes in the night air.

Two Sisters

I understand now

how when they found her
in the river

her bones still sang.

ENTELECHY

I am beginning to think that seeds
have no concept of the blooms they will
become and simply press against the dark,
spurred by an imperative of unimaginable
fullness. Could you sense it even then,
when you were empty of all the knowing
you would find unendurable later? You ached
for her, like the wings that slipped from your back
when you fell, entranced by the promise of naming.

She was a mountain, distant, heart bared to the sky,
that needed the weight of you (soft and earthbound
creature), that called the gravity of your love
to curl atop her feet
and make the cleft valley of her shadow
flower.

GIVEN

We have been given
to living.

Remember the brave dignity
of a heart that still feels

enough to break. Be
the fool in love

the saints call
to teach them to dance.

HOLOGRAM

Certainty can be tolerated if it leaves room
for possibilities as yet undiscovered. They said

if she painted black on black

no one would see the forms, and thus she learned
to speak her invisibility. What is earthly

is illusory and still

the storehouse of the real. Her body knew
that black on black was not erasure but

a hologram of unbearable intimacy,

the kind where signs spill over darkness
and then vanish,

being inextricably inside.

STAR BABY

You are a point of invisible light
inside a wound I cannot remember.

I feed you from my heart

in a wordless prayer
that is never ending.

MINEFIELD

I take a walk upon myself,
touching this flesh that has longed served
as a cocoon for all the tender,
frightened brilliance of the human heart.
My hands pass over, exploding centuries
of hidden mines, and does it matter
who buried them or why
when you are a furrow,
a raw and holy wound,
and you know
for one earth-shattering second,
as your breast is carved out like a bowl,
and the worms look like severed tongues
while they dance their blind undulations
in the shock of sudden exposure,
and your eyes engorge with the sight
of the fistfuls of time splintering the sky,
that this is something greater than transformation
or union, and you lie on your back
as the soil rains down, refusing to blink.

Earth Prayer

what is written on
your Body now

oh sweet ground

these are not
the final words

(Not) A Love Song

The sheets part like green water, broken by the arc
of hip and thigh,
rich,
round,
and voluptuous as a cello. Streetlights
have taken the place of the moon, but your skin
is still pale and white as a beginning.

You can cut down every tree, and in each man's heart
there will remain a forest
where no light reaches the ground. There, wolves prowl
with the scent of winter swirling in their nostrils,
and dragons with scales like coins jealously
guard their hordes
of forgotten jewels,
while women sleep beneath the earth,

or in towers too high
for even the gods to hear them. This body

that is mine (because it is given)
is not a love song. Our language is dead
or has never been. Your body,
that is now mine,
is a shipwreck,
and I,
the sea that claims it.

FIGUREHEAD

Ever-so-gently, she pressed her lips
against the shell of his ear and whispered,

"You are a fortress,
with moats and guards,
towers and dragons,
and an entire kingdom
plunged into forgetting."

(At night, she walked along the shore
gathering pieces of his love
from the beach where the tides had laid him.)

The angel turned his head, as though called
by a name he had long ago discarded.

"How many fish do you suppose it will require
to break the fast of our starvation?" She cut off
both her breasts and tossed them in the sea.

He rose atop the pile of flotsam she had once
adorned, fearless as it knifed its way
through unfathomable waters, and watched them
drift away from her...two white whales...
a mating of ghosts...

THE WISDOM OF EXTREME INTROVERTS

Deep is wide.

There is no outside, no inside,
simply nakedness dancing its perpetual
offering that was always, already
given away. Togetherness stings
with the isolation of reflections
that can never touch.

Dive.

The roots are found
only when they cease appearing.

SEARCHLIGHT

I am lying in the wreckage of my love.

It fans around me like a broken eggshell, shards of blue sky
and smelling faintly of stale bread.

The longing that annihilated a world is gone; now
I can only feel quiet things. I say to my heart,

"Goodness can be neither fenced out nor held in."
A passing hawk drops its shadow like a searchlight.

I am found in the dark.

NURTURE

I have spent far too many months
with death standing at the foot of the bed
or draped in virile bonelessness
against the armchair
not to know that these bodies
are but the slightest
most infinitesimal fraction
of who we are
And yet it was the insect of this body
so fragile
so small
who showed me the secret
of where my Heart had been kept safe
in every cell
and from whom I learned
the abandonment of brutality
and how to dwell in peace
amidst the roots of violence
and how to nurture without forcing
the most silent seeds
of the myriad worlds
given into our care

IMPOSSIBLE

It is impossible
to believe
in a punitive
God while
smelling
lilacs.

THE ARCHANGEL

The archangel adored the earth
and fell into a human life solely
that she might have a warm creature-belly
to press upon the ground, and arms,
if not as wide as wings, more ecstatically unfurled
in awareness of their frail brevity, to embrace it.

Sinuously, the fragrance of the grass rose
and stained her cheek as she crooned
to the smallest things,
the pebbles and roots, and the skeletons of leaves
that were once held aloft in a blaze of sap green
burned to the elemental fires of autumn's longing.

In the loamy soil beneath, a single seed
split its skin in answer,
and felt a sun it had never seen, round as a yolk,
in echo of its fullness.

PRELUDE

Rest long
in the darkness
of your fertility.

Time will arise and you
will wake

in a field of brightness.

EVE'S SERPENT

I needed to lie on the ground
and press my skin against
the moment's strangeness
and how it felt to be
too exhausted for tears
while my heart carried on
shedding itself like a snake.

(There are ways we learn to crawl again.
There are sweet ways to learn
the humility of dust.)

Tomorrow
I will wake and sing that I belong
to something fierce and alive
and that Love carried my body
on her back and breathed for me
when I was low and fell
(as angels do) into her arms.

THIS

After all of the fight has gone out, there is this:
the invitation to extraordinary tenderness.

AGAIN

Trying again
we are shy and not
as certain
of the immortality of love.
In the earliest advent
of springtime,
the river wears a cold
and broken skin.

Tragedy is overcome
through the startling
commitment
to the everyday real.

There are two suns
in the sky:
one dim, one bright.
You smile

and kiss my cheek.
The earth smells green.

DID YOU

Did you wake today
and let the sky touch you
knowing that space
is its own meaning and that blue
is an enough-ness you can walk inside
for miles and disappear

Did you kiss yourself
in the eyes of what you love
the most and thank
the time that steals the certainty
you hid in names
especially your own

Did you find
the strength in what will leave you
and the secret yes of your despair
whose cheeks and pockets bulge
like a child hoarding candy
with the unrecognized sweetness

of your abundance Did you
overflow and did I

reach out my hands
(not to save but simply) to feel

the bright spill of your fountain
blessing me?

PROCLAMATION

It is a sure sign
that feeling
has been abandoned
when we grow too precious
with our emotions.

Who among us
cannot point to someone
somewhere in our lives
and cry out
in childlike betrayal and helpless rage,
"You did not love me enough!"

Leave open the wounds
that mend through being empty.
Behind our ears, we are all
tucking cemetery flowers.

Sing. Wail. Proclaim your life.

EVEN THE SMALL

Even the small can be generous
as it gives itself away.

TRINITY

Our dismemberment took place underground
where no one could see, our crucifixion was not
public. It was too dangerous to be cheapened
into spectacle. Too dangerous
even for that.

(She had a gift for carrying people
on her back, out of hell.

She bound them together
like sheaves of wheat.

She was a harvester of souls.)

What now, love, when my hips
are wide as a blue horizon?
What now, when your tongue is a root
searching for the soil in which
my flesh dissolved?

Resurrection
is an eternal happening.

You worried that your heart
was hard but I said, No
it is as pregnant
and essential as the stone
inside a fruit.

(I remembered that her skin
smelled like an orchard.)
I opened my chest

and a fish swam away
mid-air.

JEDIDIAH

Jedidiah loved her
because she had no meaning.

Or rather, he loved her
because he understood, after long years
of crushing despair, the false starts, fantasies,
and disappointments, that the only meaning
that could touch the tear in his soul was the one
that was indecipherable. It was her irreducible
ineffability that silently redeemed the banality
and disenchantment of the world.

She traveled from nothing to nothing,
and her lips tasted the same, though she
was not. Body was a coherence of longing.
Heart was a repetition of *yes*
scrawled like a rune
on the membrane of each cell.

At night, her love would pour
out of her breast and perch atop her ribs,
swiveling its head and blinking
its bright eyes.

Jedidiah's blood raced in his sleep.
He heard the sharp snap of wings
above his head and moaned.

BLACK ANGEL

It is (I am) a late-summer bloom. There are
butterflies everywhere (surrounding me)
now. Yesterday (on our walk), a black
angel (black as a raven's claw) flew up
into my face (into the pupil of my wisdom-eye),
flash of blue before a dissolution of brightness.

ABANDON

We choose the lesser love,
but what is for us
will find us,
despite our protestations.

It is a grace

to allow someone to reveal
a sweetness hidden inside us
we have never met.

Ever

our foolishness trails behind, wondering
if we remember the joke. And so,
I would abandon any pretense

of a sober heart, whirling
untouched
by shame or consequence,
to teach you

all the steps I'd saved up

from my years of silent wanting
and the names the stars called us
as we burned

in a sky beyond despair.

LETTING GO

There are things we want to say
but don't. (Like this:) the ones we hoped
would love us but didn't don't matter
now. We have to stop trying to stretch
them to cover our holes, like a blanket
that shrunk as we grew large
and never kept us warm, although
we gave ourselves completely
to believing it did.

Say, Let go, to the world,
and to all that clings beyond its time,
and then again (in a whisper)
to yourself. Courage is a choice
and defenselessness can be
a revelation.

Say, My heart spills milk,
and know you mean

amen
amen
amen.

We Belong

We belong to more
than earth. The causeless ground
of rest swells through all activity.

Abandon self-importance.

Enter the paradox
of prostration as flight.

Only then will we embrace
the love we have been given for a time:
the breast that feeds us, the home
we gift, the home we make.

THE LAST SPARKS

I saw my goodness, and it was
simple, the way that wild things
bear their beauty. I thought

of all the times I was forced
open, because I was there
and so I believed I must.

I felt.

And the wind did not
change course, but there was
no sail to catch it. And somewhere

a woman was struck,
leaving no sound. And though we had
no voice, our hearts cried out

in falling, like the thunder of water,
or the legions of angels
we called with the last sparks of our love

that dropped,
flaming,
from the sky.

MI/ACROCOSM

Inside an atom, there are
light-years of distance.

"All intimacy is non-local," I said to the angel,
as we sat at the kitchen table sipping tea.

He cradled my naked feet in his lap.
Neither of us knew the time.

SELF-PERSEPHONE

I saw that my heart was a pomegranate,
excitation blush of underworld fruit,
and when it was cut open
by vagary and circumstance, as all hearts are,
it spilled seeds that were luminous fish eggs,
salty as tears, seeds spinning
like celestial wheels, winged and burning,
seeds of self-impregnating androgynous abundance, seeds
like hanging globes of dew,
seeds held overlong in death's cold mouth,
seeds smooth as sea glass that found
the secret beauty fused unyielding
to every violent, battered impulse, every undertow
that stole the sky, quiet, brilliant seeds
that promised countless unreflected moons.

NOT-TWONESS

And not to think (of any)
not to think
to divest oneself of sadness
any misery in the sound
to lay it down
in the sound of the wind
(to lay it down)
in the heaviness of what is ever-green
like boughs atop the snow
thick with the history of pine
and needles that prick
sucking the cherries that rise
from fingertips in the shock
of sudden wounding.

(You said) body is wind
empty and hospitable to
no one
a world where what lives here
has no arms or hands for grasping
the tenderness of the invisible
life through which light
falls.

To be so quiet
so immune to despair
so human

that you know how to hate
and lose
and love again and how I hold
in the folds of my bare palm
the promise of your beginning
and when you take my hand
two nothings press against
each other in bodiless inseparability.
(Where then do you find union?)

PROOF

There is no proof in love,
only endless, overflowing participation.

ROLLING THE DICE

She once asked him why
angels had eyelids, as they never slept
and had no difficulty gazing directly
into the sun. Stroking her cheek
with a feather in that distracted way,
he languorously drawled, "The closing
of an eye is a universe of meaning."

He rolled his dice
at her feet.

She said, "My love, every game
ends in losing it all."

Wordlessly,
he removed his wings
so they could lie together inside them,
staring up into the vault of space.

HE SAID SHE SAID YOU SAID I SAID

He said, Justice is a human ideal
with which the world rarely complies.
She said, Dance the wild fury of your love
while the angels that you cling to burn. You
grimaced, teeth gleaming like rosary beads. I said,
Suffering is not the most interesting thing about me.

He said, I wish I could feel something.
She drew a heart-shaped boat in the sand for the sea
to break. You said, I want/I don't want to be alone. I
shouted my silence.

He was a bird flying through her open
window. She said, There's a nest in a corner
of the attic and the house is filled with song.
You said, I am hiding under the pear trees, come
and find me. I bent my face close to the blades
of grass and whispered, You are my amazement.

HANUMAN THROUGH TIME

you are
every name
ever written
on my heart

ACKNOWLEDGEMENTS

I've heard it said that there is no such thing as individual salvation or enlightenment, a sentiment I believe holds equally true for any act of creation. This book exists through the extraordinary generosity and countless acts of kindness of a Body much larger than my own. I am grateful beyond measure to Ron Starbuck and Saint Julian Press for taking the chance on a new writer and allowing words born of alchemical intimacy and isolation to find a more expansive context and meaning; to Fred LaMotte for championing this connection with enthusiastic open-heartedness; to the community of helpers and healers who kept me alive through a period of critical illness long enough for me to write what eventually became this manuscript, especially Kurt Hill and Jan Iwata of Holistic Health Practice, Gary Xie of Ton Shen Health, and Lucien Caillouet.

Thank you to the late Emilie Conrad, founder of Continuum Movement, and the Words and Waves family, for giving me an unmistakable taste of what it might be like to be brilliant within a collective of brilliance; to Linda Chrisman, for listening to the bones; and to Rebecca Mark, whose advice seeded into the field of shared creativity gave me the push I needed to risk publishing my work.

To Dan Brown, Ph.D. and the Pointing Out Way, I offer boundless gratitude for imparting the foundation that stabilized a lifetime of mystical experience into a view of the limitless embodied potential of radical wisdom-love.

Thank you to my family, and in particular my parents, Glenn and Susan, whose unwavering support provided the safe space for a necessary death, and whose love kept me tethered to life.

To my Mom, from whom I learned the fierceness of devotion: Nothing I could say would ever be enough.

Finally, stunned gratitude and delight to my beloved, Kevin, for taking on the challenge and possibility of a life together in mutual adoration of the real. You are every name ever written on my heart.

And to the Angel.

Britt Posmer is a poet, visual artist, and dancer who began spontaneous image-making and writing during a period of critical illness and spiritual awakening. Her work depicts a consciousness and holistic vision that has flowered from a commitment to creative process as both devotional self-emptying and a unique expression of somatic mysticism. Originally trained as a classical ballerina, she spent nearly two decades performing and touring with various companies based in Chicago, IL, including Ballet Chicago, Ballet Theatre of Chicago/Lexington Ballet, and Chicago Ballet. Shortly before her illness in 2009, Britt received a scholarship to the School of the Art Institute of Chicago, which she attended with a focus in Performance and Visual and Critical Studies. Her last piece, "there is a way in which the body sleeps," created in collaboration with performance artists Lisa Abbatamarco and Joshua Kent, was presented as part of a collection of dance works curated by Ayako Kato at Epiphany Episcopal Church in Chicago in August 2009.

Metaphor and poetry acted as a first language during a time of initial recovery from severe PTSD in early adulthood and grew to become the most valuable and reliable form of truth-telling, a map to consciousness, and a self-clarifying window to the ground of Being. Throughout the years, what began as a journaling practice opened into an ongoing conversation with the heart of Reality, spanning both visual image and word, in contextually overlapping fields of incarnation. It has only been recently that Britt has started to share this inner experience publicly, exhibiting her paintings and gathering her poems in collected form. Her curiosity and intense love for the body suffuse her creations with a fierce vulnerability and nakedness, and a passion for the paradox at the heart of awakened embodiment.

In addition to her artistic pursuits, Britt is also a nationally certified massage therapist and a studied practitioner of shamanic healing and energy medicine. Her education includes training in Reiki, Toltec and Hawaiian shamanism, Zero Balancing, Advanced Psychosomatic Character Therapy, and Continuum Movement.

Britt was raised in the Episcopal Church, and the unitive stream at the heart of Christianity still holds a special place in her spiritual life. She is an avid student of the continuous revelation at the root of all the great wisdom traditions and has a particular passion for the reintegration of the Feminine within the language and experience of Awakening.

CPSIA information can be obtained
at www.ICGtesting.com
Printed in the USA
FSOW02n0833270217
31311FS